Heathen Hymnal

Sarah Bergwin

Presentation by *BookLeaf Publishing*

Web: www.bookleafpub.com

E-mail: info@bookleafpub.com

ISBN: 9789357214919

First edition 2022

Ortez Mountains, January

The snow turns purple
for a blink
as the last citrus streaks
drain from the sky

Lavender ink
spills across
the jagged ridgelines
A last bit of color
before the Earth
surrenders itself
to the silver
Sliver of the Moon.

Flurry

Time evaporates,
Boundaries blur

A slurring flurry
of words escapes my lips

Your reply
is a blizzard of stars

Periphery

The truth lies
At the periphery –

Skirting the edge of darkness,
Trailing the coastline
of sanity.

Strung along by starlight,
Sandy feet
Ascend
the slippery slope
of solitude.

The moon illuminates
Her own reflection,
Lucid lunar liquid,

A silent conversation,
Punctuated
By stardust.

Wet Skin

The ridges in the sand
are like Braille
Submerged, my feet read
the Lake's poetry,
Toes curling into the Lakebed,
Seeking another chapter,
A few more words at least,
From that lower, colder level.
Finding only silence,
I wade toward the horizon,
Trailing my fingers
Across the wet skin
of the water's surface,
trying to absorb Her secrets.

Somewhere Sacred

5

Stolen syllables
Ignite forgotten fires

Born from starlight,
We drink the moon's milk,
Fill our bellies with magic

Liquid love coats our tongues,
Trickles through
the space between us

Pools somewhere
silent and sacred.

Stump

The stump in the backyard
From the dead Oak tree
is saturated after yesterday's rain.
The Earth-sweet scent
of decomposition
rises in smoky tendrils.
The Oak's death
is a vaporous memory
on a moment's breeze.

Still

I see you
In the static,
Windless day

You are the
Absence
Of the wind,

The still,
Leafless branches
Tattooed
Against the ashen sky.

Rivulets

Black veins
Slice the sky
Bare branches
Waver

A breath of wind
Resuscitates
The frozen scene

The Sun,
A warm but fleeting dream
Makes rivulets
of the icebound stream

Mirror for the Sun

9

Minnows swim downstream,
their fluid bodies
bathed in silver-scaled secrets,
Slippery mirrors
for the Sun

Cosmic Dust

We are starlight -

Cosmic dust -

Loose particles
in a vast expanse

That somehow
Collide

View at Dawn

Blue sky
through empty liquor bottles
A museum
of fuzzy memories

Unwashed cast-iron
pancake pan
Soaks in the sink,
Threatening rust

Shrike

Sharp,
Shrill

Butcher bird
Sings to its kill

December Sun

We fell in love
in the trenches
of our separate despairs,
wove our wounds together
and wrapped ourselves
in a blanket of communal grief.

In your dark bedroom,
We cradled each other,
Our wet eyes
Closed tightly
Against the sharp
December sun.
The wind whispered in
Through the cracked glass
Above our bed
And lifted the curtain

Light sliced in,
Exposing the broken
Window to your soul.

Ancestors

I see your likeness
In the lichens
You speak to me
Wordlessly
Through the grooves
In the trunk of
The dying tree—

Sacred scripture
Bored into the Ash
By an emerald insect
A silent library
Inscribed
In larval language
Whispers of the soul

August's Ashen Blush

15

Death sets stage for new life -
The summer kill.
The sky, on fire
Falls into the lake's
Cold,
Wet
Embrace

December Lake

Lacy collar of ice
      rims the shore
A wave frozen
      till spring,
when the Sun will erase
      all trace,
Dissolve the snow and ice -
      a steamy defeat -
Release the waves
      to float and flow,
Again unchained

Alchemy

The Sun creates -
    He warms the frozen soil,
    Feeds the timid seedling,
    Bathes the swimmer's skin.

So, He destroys -
    Obliterates the winter's work,
    Vaporizes snowy sculptures,
    Burns the backs of forgetful bathers.

Skin and soil absorb,
    while ice and snow dissolve,
    Water accepts the raw heat and tempers it.

Joyful swimmers splash and float,
    Dive and jump, oblivious to the
    Alchemy, though they are dripping in it.

Feast

Does the tree worry
whether tomorrow it will rain?

Or does it simply rejoice
in the rippling sunlight
and feast with hungry leaves?

Blood on Our Hands

Our hands betray us -
Mine, stained with the
blood of many beets -
Yours with the harvest
of a still-warm doe

Carbon

Death releases us
from skin that scars,
Flesh that bruises,
Hands that hesitate.

Our carbon filters
and realigns -
    a breath of wind,
    a twisted pine

Our souls split
    from splintered shells
    and rise like smoke above the hills

www.ingramcontent.com/pod-product-compliance
Lightning Source LLC
LaVergne TN
LVHW050310200726
843509LV00015B/3252